Leaves from an Ancient Tree

BETTYE WAGES

Leaves From An Ancient Tree by Bettye Wages.

Copyright © 2024. All rights reserved.
Printed in USA.

No part of this book may be reproduced in any form whatsoever without written permission from the publisher or the author except in the case of brief quotations embodied in critical reviews, articles, and essays.

Cover Design and Interior & Layout Design: MyPublishedBook.com

Cover and Interior Art: Bettye Wages

ISBN: 979-8-218-49753-8 (paperback)

Table of Contents

Preface 7

Chapter 1: Nature Calling 9

The Mother Oak 10

Ancient Wisdom 12

Joy Returning 13

Spring Awakening 14

The Evening Cathedral 15

Homage 16

Falling Into New Life 17

Sunday at the Pond 18

A Pandemic Awakening 19

Just Is 20

The Lover 21

Chapter 2: The Heart Calls 23

Finding Love's Meaning 24

Love Like Water 25

Let Me See 26

Leaping Hearts 27

Soulmates 28

A Look into Loving Eyes 29

A Look into Eyes Again 30

The Gift 31

A Viral Connection 32
The Gate Stood Open (Where Love Is) 33

Chapter 3: Who am I? **35**
Seek and Ye Shall Find 36
Flirting with Chaos 39
Break Dance 41
Invisible Diadems 42
Unique 43
Unshattered 45
A Reflection 46
Age Rich 47
Searching 48
The Hike 49
If I Could 50
The Queen Reigns 51

Chapter 4: Breaking Out **53**
The Blues 54
The Tardy Visitor (Not quite finished) 55
Pulling Threads 56
Loosening the Knots 57
To My Beloved America 58
The Cracked Bell 59
A Poison Weed 61
If the Truth Be Told 62
To Thee I Sang 63
The Migrant 64

Chapter 5: Awakening **65**
Mornings of Thankfulness 66
Heavens! 68
Heaven? 69
Wisdom 70
Hope 71
A Moment 72
Eternity 73
Seeking Peace 74

Leaves from an Ancient Tree

Can't go Back 75
Impermanence 76
On and On. 78
Reading the Obits. 79
The Voice (Dad). 80
Peace Awaiting 81

Preface

For many years, I have been journaling, writing my unrelenting thoughts. Some I have finally been brave enough to call poetry. Some I call just "writing" understanding that it is all in the mind of the beholder. Being raised in Louisville, Kentucky by two loving parents that I have come to appreciate as being extraordinary in many, many ways, giving love and guidance, not only to our immediate family, but also to the extended relatives of aunts, uncles, and cousins. I was fortunate to be surrounded by three brothers who were also loving and caring and extraordinary in their own ways and a much older half- brother who never lived with us, but always left me in awe with his calm and caring demeanor. My sister for whom this lonely girl prayed nightly, finally came when I was 13 years old, baby- sitting age. She is now deceased but gave a tremendous amount of fun and love during her time on the planet.

    I am now the mother of three wonderful children and the grandmother of five and great-grandmother of two. All of whom have given me much joy and pleasure, as well as moments of anxiety and reflections, that have made me even more appreciative of my life and whatever amount of wisdom I have acquired.

Poetry

The world I see
is an extension of me.
My heartbeat, the rhythm, my breath,
the rhyme.
Poetry surrounds me,
I extend into it.
A rejoining of what has
always been.

Chapter 1
Nature Calling

The Mother Oak

Years ago, when anyone asked me where I lived, my usual response was "The house on the corner of Cecil Avenue with the big oak tree", knowing they would immediately identify the house; an ordinary house that gained a look of refinement and importance with the presence of the big oak tree. Greeting our walkway with huge, outstretched arms and keeping vigilance over our home, this stately tree stood at her post, with her usual adornment of rich green ivy.

A beautiful and charitable tree that shaded the house from the summer sun. Then as evening fell became a shimmering canopy as we sat at her feet in the moonlight. In autumn, its deep brown colors gave dramatic statements of beauty to the canvas of grey skies. The gracefully felled leaves provided a lush and crunchy carpet that brought delight to playful feet. Like an athlete with mighty arms stretched upward, it received the pounding of rains and winds and victoriously carried the weight of the winter's snow. In spring it sprouted a new frock, dressed anew to cushion and cradle the many nests in its branches... again and again, year after year, until one day the cycle stopped. The juices that had once provided her energy and suppleness were at last drained. She was no longer able to clothe herself. The branches were no longer able to withstand the weight and stress as she began to weep and break. With bowed head, quietly, majestically, she died.

The birds still flew in and around her naked arms and their babes still presented themselves to the world in her niches; but the shelter, the beauty and all that life had provided were no more.

The tree is now gone, the house left unattended, unadorned. All that remains is the stump with its tremendous disc displaying rings that tell of a lengthy life. Perhaps viewed closely by a tree expert there may be indications of various stresses and something of environmental conditions that impacted on her throughout her life, but no record of the delights she sponsored or the enhancements she gave to her surroundings. Nothing of the laughter and chatter that echoed among her branches, nor the many songs of birds long gone that provided her chirping cheerful voice. Nothing of all the millions of leaves and acorns produced and fallen, which in turn have reproduced again and again.

A grace, a comfort, a nurturing body...gone at the house where I once lived.

Ancient Wisdom

The Gingko tree stands tall.
Reaching towards heaven,
She's seen it all.

Her seeds fed the dinosaurs
that left with an impact,
destroying the lives
that had kept her intact.

She survived, still bearing fruit,
knowing a history
that only she can intuit.

So, she smiles at me.
Yellow and bright, as the sun
amplifies her majestic glee.

Her leaves, an ancient chop
signifying her wonder, her beauty.
Wisdom flowing through her veins,
gleaned from tenacity and veracity.

She fears not life's waxes
nor its wanes,
but still stands defiantly tall,
with grace and beauty,
embracing it all.

Joy Returning

This early spring day
life begins her play
stirring in its colors.

Breaking out-daffodils,
waving their flags
while standing in a yellow field.

Crocuses smiling
with a purple grin.
Saying "yes, I'm back again."

Birds, red, blue, black and grey,
singing their distinct praises,
all superior in their own way.

The varied greens now on stage
applauding in celebration
of life, ready to engage.

New beginnings in all its hues.
Just life continuing
and paying its dues.

Spring Awakening

Flowers shouting,
 "See me, see me!
Enjoy the wonder
of my adornment.
Colors vivid, dense,
soft and delicate,
dressed to dance
with the wind.

Smell me, kiss
me hold me, love me,
I am here for you.

See me, see me!
I never left you
I only took a rest,
awaiting the warmth and rain,
awaiting my time
to be with you again."

The Evening Cathedral

There is a choir singing in the quiet dusk.
A combination of chirps, buzzing
and high-pitched vibrations,
radiating from trees, the grass,
the ever-searching vines,
a chorus coming together.

Flying and fluttering things
intoning praises for the day's bounty.
Food, perhaps even a mate or two,
and still having life at the end of the day.

They may sing through the night,
 their hallelujah praises
intermingled with the amens
of more distant pray-ers.
The cosmic maestro raises its wand,
Hallelujah-Amen, Hallelujah-Amen.
The choir of nature sings.

The trees, the grass,
the flying and crawling things
all join in on their songs of gratitude.
Let Heaven and Nature sing,
Let Heaven and Nature sing.

Homage

The tree applauds the wind
passing by,
acknowledging the Adventurer,
the Conqueror, the Lover,
whose gentle kisses soothed
a sunburned heart,
then moved on.
The tree stands rooted
in admiration of the power
of that unseen
moody thing,
at times gentle and embraceable,
uplifting the wings of flying things,
and then loudly howling
just because it can,
creating chaos from which
new things evolve.
The tree bows
in homage to the wind
and in thanksgiving
that it is standing at all.

Falling Into New Life

Whirling leaves,
falling from different tribes.
Red, gold, brown,
the Ash, the Aspen,
Sweet Gum and Sycamore,
leaving their places of birth.

A retirement gala,
playing together in
a grounded jubilation.
A journey's end.
A task complete.

A terminal dance of
celebratory movements.
A spinning pointe, a waltz,
a frolicking rustle in a gentle breeze
on a waiting ground.

No discriminatory divides,
hierarchy irrelevant,
fallen stars
from their tribal roots
in oneness,
in joy,
anticipating their time of rest.

Brittle crunches under carefree feet
signals a heartfelt last goodbye.
But now, refined and redefined,
a new journey begins.

Sunday at the Pond

A pulpit of shimmering water,
a kindred of Bethesda's pool.
No books needed for pounding out messages,
no deacons, teachers or Sunday school.
A flock of swimming ducks
quack their amens and
Hallelujahs.
The fish and frogs
in perpetual baptism,
the waving fans of branches
expressing the joy of life.

The choir of chirping birds in
a vibrating organ of praise.
No shouting and stomping,
no rituals needed.
Only the blessed peace
of the gentle wind.
A place of worship
with the silent whisperings
of gratitude and thanksgiving.
A loud Thank You!
And
Amen.

A Pandemic Awakening

Is it age?
Is it just a viral slowing down?
The seclusion?
Or just a long time coming
awakening.
Allowing me
to see, to pay attention,
to what has always been
waiting for recognition,
a connection.

The grasses, their varieties,
how they grow.
The songs of birds,
how they sing.
The shadows,
how they frolic with light.
My breath, the vibrations,
the energy's connections.

I see, I hear, I invite
this shaking, this enlivening, this entrance
into a new world view.
One I mistakenly thought I knew.

Just Is

Scientist, Theologians, Philosophers
investigate, imagine, speculate,
declare and imagine again.
Its beginnings.
Its meaning.
Its ending.
Life doesn't care.
Life, the how, the what, the why
in all its many forms,
just is.
Joyously, enthusiastically,
defiantly, determined,
just is.
Energy ever morphing,
giving and receiving.
Life just is.
Over and over,
again.

The Lover

The pitter-patter of a warm rain
Gently arousing the arid earth
Sluggish from neglect,
Hardened and thirsty in waiting.

A wetness comes-
An opening exposed,
A pounding
Widening the crevices.
Drops becoming torrential,
Thunder roaring,
Lightning flashing,
Convulsions of acceptance,
A taking in of a long-awaited embrace
Climaxing in a fullness,
An expansion.

A welcoming rejuvenation,
A longing, a hunger
Received,
Satisfied.

Chapter 2
The Heart Calls

Finding Love's Meaning

Love is a word from a foreign land,
Yet spoken in the hearts of all,
It arises from the places
One has journeyed, or longs to go.
Love says:
Come go with me, to the bottom of our oceans,
Finding the pearls of long ago wounds
And the ones still in the making.
Cruise with me across an ocean, peaceful and turbulent,
Fly with me over invisible terrain that can only be imagined.
Love says:
Come, let us learn the language together,
Speaking the tongue known from childhood,
And defined by life.
Come, take my hand,
Let us travel together.
There are places yet to go,
We will develop our own code,
A new syntax rising up in meaning
Like smoke from a blazing fire
Then resting as cool vapors
On a distant but novel land.
Love says:
Come, let's learn the depth of this spoken word,
Let there be no foreign tongues here.

Love Like Water

Water wets the dry places,
seeping in crevices and deep holes.
A droplet rising from an ocean
vaporizes and invades
whatever unshielded thing it touches.
The ferocious waves,
and the gentle flows
sometimes renews
sometimes drowns.
Much like that thing,
that energy,
that indescribable thing known as
Love

Let Me See

Let me see through the eyes of love
all things
and then I will see you.
Let the veil of your luminous presence
be like lenses
before my eyes.
The light that is yours
illuminating each object from within—
shining outward.
Let my eyes see you
in every soul.
Let my love see you
in me.

Leaping Hearts

My heart quickened when first we met
as if it had discovered a long-lost love.
It was the heart that leaned towards you
as a flower leans towards the sun,
knowing there is good and life to be had
if only in the connection could be made.

My heart leaps towards your spirit anticipating
the embrace that awaits.
A recognition that stands in awe.
A commitment-that is what the heart made,
without consulting anyone,
not even me.

Soulmates

Did we know each other a thousand years ago?
My soulmate,
did we run and play in an ancient sun,
fly kites, blow bubbles?
How many times before
have you held my hand,
calmed my heart,
excite my soul?

What depth have we not yet reached
that brings us back again?
What smile, what kiss, what tear,
what love yet unexpressed?

How many times will we
find each other in times and places
yet unknown?
New gender, new shell,
yet still,
Playmates,
Lovemates
Soulmates
Friends.

A Look into Loving Eyes

Eyes that pull in and wrap around the world
giving up everything open and pure.
A mesmerizing blessing
giving peace, pleasure, excitement,
and a million years of knowing.
Electric at the surface.
Spiritual at its depth.
Who but thee, who but us?
To peer into eternity and see God.
To see all our past lives.
To see the child that was
and continues to be.
To see the wisdom that maturity brings.
To see the love that only God can give,
Magnetic and powerful,
fuel for my soul.

A Look into Eyes Again

Eyes set deep,
reaching back into the comfort of
the womb.
The wisdom of the soul
shielded by felt lashes
reluctant to the exposure
of compassion
taking place around them.
Protected, yet piercing as néedles,
critical, accusing, frightened,
alone.
Eyes that see the universe yet remain blind.
As absorbing as the cosmic black holes,
sucking up everything and giving up
nothing,
making cold and gravity laden
all things in its orbit.
Beauty invisible,
gentleness, becoming painful
specks of suspicious dust,
leaving blind,
a fearful injured heart.

The Gift

Silence gave me your life anew,
when I can hear your voice inside of me,
when I can see you everywhere around me,
when your touch is felt everywhere at once.

Stillness gave me you,
in every thought, memory and vision.
Gave me you in recaptured times
of music and laughter.
Silence, stillness, broke down walls,
took away the divide
and gave me you.

I can go forward and take you with me,
knowing in silence and stillness
that which had been blurred, hidden, and smothered.
The fullness of life is once again ours,
renewed, whole and alive.

A Viral Connection

I went to visit my friend today.
We sat in the shade of several tall trees,

being sure we were at least
six feet apart.

Masked, and shielded we talked
about moments of anxiety,
the uncertainties of life,

the certainty of death.

A mild breeze reminded me
of the certainty of change,
as shadows were cast
by the dance of leaves.

Yes, shadows dance.

My friend's eyes smiled.
Feet became inches as
joy became our shield.

We embraced
and proclaimed
without
anxiety or fear,

"What a beautiful,
beautiful day!",
and thank you
for being my friend.

The Gate Stood Open
(Where Love Is)

His name was Pet,
that's what we were told
he was.
Brown eyes, no pedigree attached,
long tail wagging with joy
while lapping table scraps.
He was our pet,
sometimes our pillow
and playmate.

One day he was gone.
No one saw him leave.
The gate stood open.
Waiting became our constant game.

He had to return,
he just had to, we thought.
We were children,
time went by slowly then.
We waited -We waited.

The day finally came, many weeks later.
He came back,
dirty, limping, scarred and bony too.
Where had he been? what battles fought?
Ready for healing he came where love was.
Never again to roam.

The gate stayed open.

Chapter 3
Who am I?

Seek and Ye Shall Find

It has been said by philosophers and scientists, that whatever is true of the universe must also be true of the individual, being some part of that whole, with each partaking of the all- encompassing universal nature to the degree it is revealed to them. I believe that everything is here to teach and enhance us. The Universe is a book of life with a zillion pages and it is available and free. Taking the time to observe and reflect on the gifts of nature around us, we can learn all we need to know, not only about other things and people, but mostly about ourselves. When doing this, somehow, miraculously, the other things can often reveal themselves as us.

As an example, several years ago I attended a wonderful workshop in Sedona, Arizona, a very beautiful and I would say, an enchanting place. One of the exercises during the workshop required the participants to go to this very beautiful natural park and to sit alone with our notebooks. We were to see what we could glean from the experience but, particularly we were to look for the Spiritual qualities like compassion, love, service, and healing wherever we might find it. We were then required to share our findings with each other when we returned in the evening.

This turned out to be one of the most enlightening experiences of the entire week. Among other things, I learned that inanimate things in the park like the grass, trees and rocks need not have tongues to speak and they have powerful messages. I would like to share with you what I found that afternoon.

From the pages of my notebook, this is what was spoken to me.

Message from the creek - I am sitting on a rock a few feet above a creek. It appeared to be mostly still except for the occasional leaf that floated by and the sound of its movements flowing against rocks and over small cliffs. As I watched, it is saying to me "my lesson to you is to be steady, to flow and find peace in the movement. It says to me, "I am those qualities you seek, "come drink from my cup. Those who do will not thirst but will find everlasting life, for I will never not be. There may be a future when some might say, "she has dried up; there used to be a stream here." But that will be an illusion, I will be forever in streams not yet birthed, in oceans and lakes; in snow, rain and fog, the clouds in the sky. I will even be in the blood that flows in the veins of your children and their children. You will not know me because I will not be as I was, but I will be, forever.

Message from the rock - My next focus was on the great red rocks. The Rocks stood with determination, they have their arms folded across their chests, they have taken a stand and will not be moved. Jutting high into the clear cloudless sky that looks like an upside-down pool, they seem to point the way for an Eagle soaring into the sky's depths—deep, into its abundance. The rock stands as if pointing to them, saying "higher! higher still!". What do these rocks know? They have stood in attention for thousands of years, weathering all the elements, watching and listening. What have they seen, what have they heard? Did they simply know to trust the earth with its shifts, quakes and floods?

They certainly know patience. They stand and wait for what and who ever comes its way. They have faith, knowing the right things will come at the right time. They simply wait. They know honor. They honor those that are in awe of their existence. They honor the snakes and coyote that play in and out of its crevices. They honor the land that lies in its shadows. They request that we honor them, to enjoy them with the dignity and respect that they deserve by right of their existence. They are proud yet give permission to those who step on its ground, to pull its flowers, to pick up its pebbles and

to build fleeting structures at its feet, though they are rarely asked. The rocks shout to me "I am about intention;

I am the way steady and sure! My mere existence is my gift.

The grass speaks—I am grass, I am tall, short, fat and thin. I have been used to make baskets, cradles, boats and bridges. I am used on roof tops for shelter and shade. I am eaten for nourishment by God's larger creatures and some maybe not so large. I can be walked on, stomped down and rested upon, but still, I rise again and again. Resilience, strength, usefulness, nourishing, I am grass, am I not Devine? I have those qualities you are seeking and that anyone would be grateful to own.

Chapter 3: Who am I?

The tree wants recognition—The tree stands staring at me with her arms open wide. If anyone is Christly, certainly I Am. I have many gifts that I give willingly and with love. I stand as one of the important nurturers of Earth. I give safety and shelter to many animals and can feed them as well. I am the backbone for great buildings and the substance of tissue paper. I give of myself fully as fuel for warmth. I have not stood as long as the rocks, but i have certainly been pounded by winds and rain and have learned to bend and flex. To your delight I can stand before you naked, proud and without shame and then change my clothes with the rhythms of the seasons, my leaves swaying in the breeze with the abandon of Salome's seven veils. Each of my branches extends to you a gift of love.

Then Weed comes into view and speaks her truth—with an attitude—You call me weed! Okay, if that's what you want to call me, but I know who I am. Same one that made you made me. Same one that gave you purpose? Well guess what, I have a purpose too. You don't really know me. You don't give yourselves a chance to know me or nurture me. You pull me up from my roots and cast me aside saying I'm crowding out your precious flowers. Well, I have flowers too, some just as pretty as any you've ever seen. They come in all colors and hues and they wave in the wind just like your precious tulips and roses. And have you noticed how hard I am to get rid of? After all the pulling and cutting and chemicals, I can jump right back up. And you won't catch me crying about hard times either. No, no, l thrive on it. Give me a hard ground, a rock, a place where nothing else grows and there 'll be. Now, can you beat that!? So don't you look down on me, and don't feel sorry for me either, I don't need your pity, 'cause I know who I am, and that's something you need to find out. Devine qualities? Well, I am full of it.

So, the Creek, the Rock, the Grass, the Tree, the Weed, all had something for me that day. They all expressed their worth, their divinity, their oneness, their love, not with words, but simply by being. And whether what I heard from them reflected my own inner awareness of self, or the energy they were giving me or a mixture of both is unclear. All I know is I was spoken to that day. I was given an opportunity to reflect on the question "who am I?"

Flirting with Chaos

I love to dance.
Listening to the rhythm of the music I hear,
making my body move to an inner flow
of synchronized movements.
A satisfying experience that keeps
music from becoming noise
as it filters inward to my bones,
causing the muscles to harmonize and hum
with the vibrating beat of the heart's magic drum.

Not too fast, not too slow,
stay with the beat, kick up my heels,
leap across the room, calmly sway.
Staying with the flow,
playing with the motion of the Universe,
the rhythm that is mine.

I watch other's dance,
realizing quickly, they are hearing
a different beat.
Yet, they seem unaware as they move
to the rhythms they hear.
They sway, jump and create,
having a wonderful time, it seems,
dispensing their energy in a frenzy
to something I cannot hear,
I cannot feel.

Dare I try their dance?
It looks easy.
They seem to enjoy it.
I take one imitating step and then another.

I become like a brittle leaf blowing in a cold wind.
Their rhythms in my ear
become a confusing cacophony
and I become a puppet
on disconnected strings.
Moving, but not dancing.
No longer me, no joy, no glee.

I was left with the stress
of making a mess,
when I only had to dance
and be me.

Break Dance

Breaking out of cells,
confined too long.
A blithe spirit frolicking
with a ray of light.
I have a song to sing,
a dance to dance.
Angels stop midair to listen,
Jitter bugs pay attention,
purpose embedded in each movement,
meaning in every note.

Opening all doors and windows,
fresh air pushing out the
putrid stale, breads of life
long molded over.
Eggshells walked on for far too long,
now become a stomping on concrete.
Old mores, old imprints
now replaced by new variations.
My songs made of major and minor keys
tilt into movements
that finds its grace only
in my embrace.

Invisible Diadems

Oh, the fragility of office,
garments and titles!
They can be given,
earned, bought
and taken away.
They are the covers,
often, the weak breakable
wrappers so eagerly sought.
Demanding an entrapped soul
to play a role,
seeking the applause,
avoiding the boos
from those controlling and
assigning the part.

Attention given to the diadem,
but where is the soul of the manikin?
"Live up to my demands" they say.

In truth,
I can only live up to my naked role,
the one enshrined in an unclad soul.
Running free, no heavy robe or crown,
where the worth of me
is truly found.

Unique

There is no one quite like me,
is there?
No one before or after.
I am unique and special.
A wonder, a blessing,
a creative expression of love.
Like all others?
Not quite..
I am different.

I will do my task in a way
that results from me
being the me
that I am,
the who-ness of me.
No one speaks like I do,
smiles like I do,
feels like I do,
moves like I do.
Not quite.

My "Good mornings"
are different from all other "Good mornings,
because it is spoken by me.
Spoken with a feeling,
a voice,
a thought,
a dimension of love,
a total expression
that only I can have.

No, no one impacts others
quite the way that I do.
The "I" that touches others
is momentous, is special,
because there is no other "I"
that makes the difference
only I can make.

In all the Universe,
no two leaves,
no two flowers
no two blades of grass,
no matter how closely they resemble
are the same.
They need not be,
The creator is efficient that way.

You who now read my words
are you not unique?
And as the I that I am
meets the you that you are,
we can be unique together.
We can begin to recognize our true identities
through oneness of spirit.
The same spirit expressed in infinite
Uniqueness.

Unshattered

Casting stones at the woman
in the mirror
shatters glossy smooth surfaces
molded in the heat of life's flames.

A truth is revealed in its many pieces.
Cutting edges, never before
exposed, acknowledged,
or embraced.

Hold her close with the
Wisdom shield.
Smooth the shards into
dull memories.
She meant well.
She learned much.
She reflects the lessons
of her transgressions.

The eyes of the beholder
holds the wisdom.
Surviving stones and storms,
she rises intact.
A presence, touched,
but not shattered.

A Reflection

Cold creams and vanishing sheens
to wipe away the maps of life's
most exciting journeys—
lines that were held
and lines that were crossed.
Bags accompanying eyes that were
the vision of youthful dreams
have now become satchels
Impossible to unpack.

Mirrors yield only an external reflection.
Bouncing off impenetrable surfaces
unable to peer into
My strength.
My memories.
My life.
My pleasures.
My regrets.
Sheltering deeply inside where no vanishing
creams or other schemes
can disperse, destroy or erase.

Age Rich

I am privileged to have been on this planet for 80 plus years. There are people in this youth centered culture, abhorring aging except for cheeses and fine wine. There are many who don't like telling their age for fear they will be treated differently, looked upon as weak or incompetent.

But me? I want everyone to know my age, my treasure of life. I want them to know,

That when they see the age lines, the intricate designs of wrinkles and interestingly placed spots, it's not because of drug abuse, alcohol, poor diet or mental stresses, but it is simply life in the process of completing an extraordinary piece of art.

I want them to know,

That when they peer into these less than bright eyes graced with gentle puffs and bags they are peering into a reflection of life's plays and dramas known by heart and that under my beautiful graying dome is a wealth of experience I have translated into wisdom.

I want them to know,

That I have heard all the jazz, operas, rhythms and songs that became the platform and soul of their beats and hip-hops.

I want them to know,

That when I forget a name, a date, or some detail, it's because I have a brain that has more memories than it is now necessary to hold.

I want them to know,

That when my feet ache, it's because of the miles I've walked and not because my shoes are too tight or my heels too high.

I want them to know,

That when I put my hands on my hips and let my back bone slip, I am not playing the game from my youth, but it's because I have been carrying around a precious body for a very long time and have learned to turn walking into a dance that I call the Hallelujah Strut.

This is me enjoying my accumulated wealth with an ever-growing appreciation for my years.

Searching

Looking outward
for the thing
embedded inside,
the gold nugget
implanted at inception.
All the religions of the world,
their practices, prayers and songs,
seeking and beseeching,
ignoring the internal
Jacob's ladder,
aligning with the truths
of life's ups and downs.

The internal, eternal,
making peace with life
and its soul mate death.

The Hike

The mountains are plentiful,
sprinkled throughout the land,
some with tiny peaks,
others surpassing the summit's stand.

Did I remember to wear my hiking boots,
the ones with the spikes digging in?
Or did I only wear my slippers
floppy and thin,
sliding me down shadowy valleys
deep, dark and hidden
taking me to places long forbidden.

Did I think to bring my insulated wind-proof jacket
with a compass in my pocket?
Or am I insisting on wearing that flimsy dress,
the one so easily given to stress?

Did I think to bring that lifesaving rope
made of the constant threads of
wisdom and hope?

Did I include in my backpack
those precious memories
for the much-needed energy snack.

Looking back on where I've been,
the journey not yet complete,
I take my time, there is no race to win.

As I listen to my beating heart,
I remain exceedingly grateful
for my wonderful ancient start.

If I Could

I would be the wind, a gentle breeze
caressing the masses,
a lover of sorts, who kisses and flees.

I would be in the laughter or children,
while propelling their colorful kites,
lifting all flying things to new and wonderous heights.

I would be the constant traveler,
unlimited by distance, mountains or oceans.
I would be the powerful energy
of change and motion.

I would be the twirling dancer
in the twisting tornado,
and the mighty giant
in the rampant typhon's blow.

I would rest in the laps
of the ocean's beaches,
playing in the world's
vast outer reaches.

Being both feared and loved,
never an end,
I would be
the Wind.

The Queen Reigns

I am woman.
I have no need to roar
to soar.
I fly on the truth of my existence.
I simply let Me be.
With all the majesty
of royalty,
I anoint this life.
I embrace the energy
of the wind, the rain,
the hurricanes.
I am their microscopic twin.
I twirl, I dance, I laugh,
I swoon, I cry.
I am woman.
Let the Queen
preside.

Chapter 4
Breaking Out

The Blues

The Blues, an expression
of depression.
The plangent calls from a broken vine seeking its way
in hopelessness
and in darkness.
Broken from its roots,
yet, seeking light,
knowing it is there.
Moaning and weeping,
still with a seed of hope lingering.
If I sing it loud enough,
if I cry it hard enough
if I can grasp this thing called faith,
so broken and hard to hold.
Perhaps, just maybe,
the yellow color of light will seep its way through sorrow,
turning the Blues into shades of green.
Indicating at last,
an acceptance of growth,
an acceptance of
Life.

The Tardy Visitor (Not quite finished)

One single tear,
where did you come from?
Why do you sit there
blurring my vision?
One single tear,
why didn't you come
while your many companions
were here?
They've done their job and gone:
Ran through my anguished heart,
flushed my soul.
That party is over,
Why do you linger?
There is nothing more
here to feed on.
You have no business here.
Your tardy pity wakes my dream.
Go away, I don't need you
now.

One single tear.
Did you hold back
thinking you were not welcome?
Why do you think I need you
now?
Dare you haunt me!
Dare you sit there like
a mirror reflecting my soul
for all to see.
Go! Begone quickly!
Please go,
I don't need you
anymore.

Pulling Threads

Pull the threads
of opinion,
and a new world appears.
Captured in past years fashion,
wearing Grandma's dresses
may be familiar and comfortable,
but not made for this season's dance.

Pull those threads.
Untie the corset.
Be in this world
unfolding.
Iron out stubborn creases.
Pull the threads.
Loosen up.
Rip and flow.

Loosening the Knots

I was told many "should nots"
even "shall nots"
from my earliest beginnings.
And then I was told I could not,
was allowed not,
get in trouble if I did.
So, I tested some "should nots"
that lead me to out step
some "could nots".
I found the cages of
Couldn't and Shouldn't
and even the "Shall nots"
were made of bars with openings, '
big enough to squeeze through.
I emerged, despite a blister or two
much wiser, much stronger
more knowing
the "nots" that I can.

To My Beloved America
(Remembering George Floyd)

Are you having a Little Trouble Breathing Today?
Is your breath seeping away?
I mean the breath you've been breathing
that left a vacuum in the breath of a people
whose lives you used to inhale the lie of your superiority?
Did you need that extra air because
you were feeling inadequate somehow?
Did you need it to induce a high that would keep you
from facing your low?
Or was it just plain greed?

Are you now feeling some of your air slipping away?
Will the day come when you scream "I can't breathe!"
as you drown in the reality of your hubris;
as you awaken to the nightmare you created?
Will you be asphyxiated by the reality
of your inhumanity and ignorance?
As you gasp for air will you call out "Mother!"
asking for more intoxicating Kool-Aid?
Or will you use that breath
to take an eight-minute and forty-six seconds
look in the mirror
and at last, breathe on your own?

Air is free.
Let us all inhale our freedom.
Let us exhale our fears.

The Cracked Bell

Sweet land of liberty,
land of the fearful,
afraid to be free;
the second amendment
more sacred than any creed.
"Thou shall not" commandments
ignored and deplored.
Guns, assault weapons,
bullets, tools of conquerors or
tools of fools,
the paranoid and the angry?

A people afraid of its projected shadows
What is in the hearts of man?
The shadow knows.
I will kill them before they kill me.
Were they ever thinking of doing that?
Were they even thinking of you at all?

Worshipers, shoppers, protesters,
schoolchildren murdered!
The sacrificial lambs of a nation
unable to rest under the cover of lies.

My country tis of thee,
Sweet Land where no one is free.
Where truth is buried
awaiting its long journey
to experience
the life, long guaranteed.
Where triggers are being pulled
on those with no defense,
while we sit blindly by
waiting for the next offense.

Wake up my citizens!
Ring the cracked bell!
Be delivered from this nightmarish Hell!
With memories short,
but long on speeches intoning
heartfelt cares,
we sit and wait
until the next senseless
massacre occurs,
to unleash another
action anemic round
of thoughts and prayers.

A Poison Weed

A lie dropped on the fertile soil
of ignorance,
takes hold and grows and grows,
becoming strong and stronger
no matter how wrong.

Evidence abounds,
to be interpreted and misread
as the planted mistruth
grows on what it is fed.

Like a weed overgrowing
the once vital flower
of truth,
it takes over the minds of community
and nations,
rooting underground,
infesting and destroying
all that was sound.

Yet, the perennial flower of
candor and consistency,
that thing that will always rise again,
sits waiting to bloom when Lies' time
finally comes to its end.

If the Truth Be Told

The most truthful words ever uttered are
"I don't know".

The rivers flow into oceans,
oceans taste the edges of continents,
savoring much, spreading much.
Yet, their truths would still say
"I don't know".

Blowing over shifting sands,
mighty winds destroying lands.
Gentle breezes visiting millenniums,
yet, in clearing would still declare,
"I don't know".

Illusions cry "liar!"
Still, unfolding truth says yet,
"I don't know".

Wisdom expressed.

Changing, evolving, imagination,
calculation, speculation,
denying itself.
Time pointing its finger to
a morphing truth–

"I don't know".

To Thee I Sang

The elementary school kid, singing
in front of the large roll down map
and a flag on the wall.
Hand over heart, loud and clear
I bellowed, "my country tis of thee".
An odd name for a country I thought,
must have been a biblical thing.
But, whatever it meant, it was okay
because it was about a sweet land
and served something called liber tea,
something I had yet to drink.

The pilgrims had caught something called pride
because they weren't around anymore,
and my father hadn't died.
So, I sang loud and clear,
having no idea what a
"Star spangle banner" was either.
But the melodies were fun and easy.
So, to thee I sang.
To the map? the flag?
No, to myself,
and the words didn't matter.

The Migrant

Dust, once in the moist cover
of living things,
dances and twirls in the
beams of rays,
searching for a home,
where none is final.
A delicate thing, a perpetual traveler.
Earth's dandruff
and keeper of invisible
secrets.

Seeking rest,
the adventurer,
the unsettled migrant,
perpetual and stubborn,
riding the strong winds
and the casual breeze,
floats away gleefully
when it causes a sneeze.

Chapter 5
Awakening

Mornings of Thankfulness

JANUARY 9, 2021

I am thankful for this morning, the sun, the wind, the chill, the possibilities that are looming, waiting for realization. I am thankful for the shadows on the wall, reminding me of how important perception and reflection are in my life. I am thankful for memory, the ability to recall the joyful, pleasant fun times which alleviate or boost up what could easily slide into sorrows and regrets. I am thankful for my children who continue to give me lessons and opportunities for reflection and opportunities to become a better parent, a better person.

    I am thankful for each of my grandchildren and their mothers. I am grateful for the things that are causing me to strengthen my compassion, the pandemic, the insurrection at the Capital Building, and even our 45th president all reminding me how precious and precarious stability can be and the importance of truth and the need to be steadfast in my faith.

    For all of this I am truly thankful.

JANUARY 11, 2021

What will this day hold? How many gifts, lessons, joys? They will be imbedded in every moment, but will I be able to recognize them? So, I give thanks for the knowing of blessings, I give thanks for each moment, for the all. I know that as events are unfolding, many will appear terrible, but these too I believe will evolve into the goodness that is everywhere present, needing only time and faith.

JANUARY 12, 2021

I am thankful for each moment. I am thankful to be able to have this feeling of gratitude. I am grateful for the understanding of the advantages of forgiveness and letting go of things I cannot change. I am grateful for the capacity to forgive others, yet realizing the most difficult kind of forgiving is self-forgiveness. Not merely justifying, but real forgiveness, the kind that comes with the realization of my innate humanness imbedded with fears, ego, and the feelings of having many yet unmet needs. Being in the world, but not of the world, is a challenge. I am grateful for the journey.

Heavens!

I am told the streets
are paved with gold.
Dangerous when wet!
But then, I would have wings,
that can fly like a jet—
growing right out of my back!!
The thought brings a pain like an ingrown toenail
with each imagined flap.

They say I will have a
diet of milk and honey,
for an eternity, it's said.
No fried chicken,
no collard greens and cornbread!!?

And a long white robe,
no frills, no laces,
no wearable art
to show off my graces.

But, you will see God
and your loved ones there,
with utmost sincerity
they solemnly swear.

But, I ask,
what about God and my loved ones here?
The God and people I hold so dear?
If I haven't found my Heaven in this place,
I surely can't imagine finding it there.

Heaven?

Heaven, a welcoming place it's said,
that comes as a reward after you're dead.
But what about the heavens here
that beckons us away from fear?
Not dying, but awakening.
Not fleeing, but embracing.
Seeing the paradise around me
dancing in the light of immortality.
Awakening to abundance and beauty,
Hallelujah shouts from budding flowers,
the milk and honey that moonlight showers.
Heaven says I am here, I never left you.
Return, return, I'm just a point of view.

Wisdom

How wise it is to know,
when to sit tight,
and when to let time
take care of the fight.

To let the lights from
Day and Night take hold
revealing the knowing
of what was never told.

White knuckles clasping
to distorted dreams,
but few things ever are
what it had seemed.

Life unfolds, clutches
and release.
Enjoy the excitement
of the changing tide.
Wisdom and mirth sit
closely, side by side.

Hope

An engine pulling
me forward
tugging me out of ruts,
drawing to my heart
energy and excitement.
Opening a path
to the unseen,
infusing imagination.
It's the Butterfly
flapping its wings,
making life happen
as an ever-renewing adventure,
giving life to Life.

A Moment

Wading in filtered water,
A retreat from a roller coaster
that doesn't need my scream.
Fear, a smoke screen
dissipated,

I swim in my infinity pool
of silence.
I hear a trash truck disposing
yesterday's treasures.

I hear the whistle of a train,
going, going, gone.
A dog barks
in the far away distance.
A moment of solitude.
A settling,
a quickening,
clothed in peace.
Immerged
in
Grace.

Eternity

Moments steadily growing,
living in gathered nanoseconds
known as time.
The swirl of the Earth's turnings
marking a life by minutes
that grow into eons.
History captures it all,
not in the remembered
or the written,
but in the evolution of life energies,
becoming the substance
of the universe.
All destined to live and evolve
In time.

Seeking Peace

Be still.
Peace is looking for you.
Floating on storm clouds
just above your head.

Be still.
In droplets of rain,
in the midst of confusion,
Peace is waiting to
to embrace you.

The winds have knocked
down doors.
Peace stands
just inside, ready.

Be still, be found.
Turn your umbrella upside down.
Let yourself be taken
not shaken.
Relax, be still.

Open your eyes.
Be found.

Can't go Back

Ah, the good old days!
"Can't wait to get back to normal".
While appearing static,
I am stuck in a memory's past
that never was.
There is
no time,
no days
no "use ta bees",
only change.
The sun rises and sets.
Clouds darken,
hovers in a slow dance and flees.
What was, is always gone.
Memories, changing with every recall,
unbeknownst to the thinker.
Embrace the new of each moment,
which is the best gift I've ever had
after all.

Impermanence

Life, a simple transient thing.
To fathom that all I see and know,
that all my memories both those
I fear and those I hold dear
are simply
This,
This,
This
Moment

Gone in an instant.
Replaced by its kin called Next.
Like clips in a movie reel,
rapid changes
making the movie
making the story.

Changes,
Changes,
Changes,
ever occurring,
never fully known,
slouching towards growth
moving towards extinction.

This moment,
This,
This,
This.
Fleeting, gone before
a thought is complete.
This moment,
this minute piece of time,
 elusive, yet real—the only reel
to be had.
In a collection of instants
I live
I Feel.
The time,
perpetually
Now.

On and On

Energy waves making what I call me
and you and everything in between.
My body and yours,
a continuous round of remaking.
Elements made of positive
and negative poles,
energy coming together,
recreating, never destroyed.

Infinity bounded by finiteness,
continuously radiating.
Perception is the only limitation.
As endless as the universe,
creativity prevails,
molding, sculpting, evolving.
The spark of a star
holds history in its fire,
giving light to life
yet to emerge.
Where then, is mortality?

Reading the Obits

Passed away. Gone home.
We will meet again one day.
This place no more
to roam.

Left the planet.
Called away to be with the Lord.
Now receiving
their long-awaited reward.

Received their wings.
Slipped the surly bounds.
Escaped Earth's stings.
Succumbed to illness.

Departed this life.
Walked into Glory
no more strife.

Gone from labor
to eternal rest.
Finished the final test.

And other versions of diversions.
Avoiding that word of dread
that frightens and saddens
when either heard or read.

But, after all is done and said,
 they are simply,
lovingly,
dead.

The Voice (Dad)

Dad's voice could carry debate
well into the night.

Never meeting a stranger,
he carried conversations
with whomever he might.

A voice that could soothe
any hurt or ill plight,
with a hug and a squeeze
it could put your mind at ease.

With a sincere look right in the eyes
his voice could encourage
and well advise.

A booming voice
with hearty laughter
it carried a strength
giving solace to disaster.

His voice carried weight
for family and friends,
but for all its brawn and wisdom too,

This voice, for the life of him
could not carry a tune.

Peace Awaiting

Find Peace
Make Peace
Never hiding,
Never unmade,
But waiting in a Blinding light
For those who dare to don
The clear lenses of
Truth, of faith, of love.

Yes, that word love,
Used over and over
Yearning for its partner Peace,
As a balance, As a filter.

Peace on a Christmas card,
Peace on a banner,
Unable to bleed itself
Into hearts wrapped
In the cloaks of anger and fear.
Peace doesn't pull the trigger
Nor does it explode bombs.
Peace is simply here, there,
Everywhere,
Waiting for its chance.
Its day in the sun.

Bettye Wages is a creative spirit who has explored various artistic pursuits, including ceramics, photography, painting, jewelry making, macramé, sewing, and more. Through these endeavors, she has sought to understand and illuminate the creative life we all share. Throughout her artistic journey, she has consistently journaled and written, only recently recognizing that some of her writings might be poetry. At the age of 85, Bettye decided to share these rhythmic thoughts and feelings in her debut poetry and essay collection, Leaves from an Ancient Tree.

Bettye earned a degree and certificate in Medical Technology from the University of Louisville. After leaving her hometown of Louisville, Kentucky, she worked at Children's Hospital, Walter Reed Army Hospital, and eventually at the NIH Clinical Center in Clinical Pathology Hematology, where she became the Hematology supervisor. While working and raising three children with her husband, she earned a Business Degree from the University of Maryland. After retiring from NIH, she pursued a master's degree in counseling psychology from Bowie State University, a field she loved and worked in for twenty-one years before retiring again.

She now lives in Lanham, Maryland, enjoying time with family and friends while continuing her exploration of the intricate creative process of life.

Printed in the USA
CPSIA information can be obtained
at www.ICGtesting.com
LVHW020601071224
798551LV00002B/282